Marxism: The Faded Dream

A Christian Manifesto

Marxism: The Faded Dream

A Christian Manifesto

Joseph Ton

Marshalls

Marshalls Paperbacks
Marshall Pickering
3 Beggarwood Lane, Basingstoke, Hants, RG23 7LP, UK
A subsidiary of the Zondervan Corporation

ISBN 0 551 01312 5

Typeset by Brian Robinson, North Marston, Bucks.
Printed in Great Britain by
Richard Clay (The Chaucer Press) Ltd, Bungay, Suffolk.

Introduction

When I was studying at Oxford (1969–1972), the Christian-Marxist dialogue was still going on in some places in the West, in spite of the deadly blow it had received in Prague in 1968, when the Soviet tanks expressed loudly and clearly what the ultimate argument of the Marxist side really was. I wasn't at all convinced that the real Marxists – the ones who hold the power – were willing to talk with the Christians. It had been made clear to us in our courses on Marxism in the Romanian universities that Christianity was doomed to disappear, and that the State was using all its educational, cultural, and propagandistic means to make it disappear as soon as possible.

Shortly before I was due to return to Romania, in 1972, I received a letter from an old Romanian Baptist leader who was then in Rome. He was a man of integrity, who never compromised his faith, and, because of his uprightness, had to suffer a lot from the communists. He explained to me that the Romanian economy was facing big problems, and that the top priority of Romanian foreign policy was to pursue a course of strong friendship with the West, especially England and the United States. He was approached by the Romanian authorities and asked if he could help with his personal contacts in the Baptist world.

He told them that he could indeed do much, if only the Romanian State would stop harassing the Baptists and give them real freedom. The authorities seemed open to discussing this issue, but they wanted him to prove that his contacts were still active, and that he could still deliver some promising diplomatic openings. This was how he came out of Romania and why he was in Rome at that time. The purpose of his letter was to make me aware that the Romanian authorities were open to a dialogue with the Baptists because of Romania's economic problems and the Baptists' diplomatic potential.

This was what started me on a series of attempts at dialogue with the Romanian authorities. As soon as I arrived home, I started to write different papers about the basic grievances of the Romanian Baptists, and I tried to convince different authorities at various levels that solving our problems would be beneficial to the whole country.

In March, 1974, I was having such a discussion with a man who had an important government position in Bucharest. At one point, he surprised me with this forthright statement: 'Mr Ton, I am a Jew. You are a Baptist. We are both minority people in this country. You know that the majority are Eastern Orthodox. Even the Communist Party leaders who declare themselves atheists still say that they are

Eastern Orthodox, for, as they say, "We are not pagan, are we?"

'And you know that the Eastern Orthodox Church insists that they are the ones who have shaped the soul of the nation and that they are the ones who have preserved her unity through the centuries, while they accuse you, the Baptists, of breaking this unity, and bringing alien influences into the nation.

'Now when you come to the communist rulers with your petitions for more rights, they look at you through the eyes of these prejudices and see you as an intruder and as a destructive, alien force. You should aim at changing this perception. Could you convince these rulers that you are bringing something good to the nation?

'You must have some good. But you have to define it. You should not come to these rulers empty-handed, just begging for the right to exist here. You have to come with a great contribution and on that basis claim the right of existence.

'Let me give you a clue. You know I am a lawyer, and a member of the bar association. In one of our meetings with the Minister of Justice, we were told that concern about the great increase in juvenile crime was the reason for commissioning a sociological study of different categories of youth to discover where the trouble came from. One of the findings of this study was that when they analysed the different religious groups, they saw, to their surprise, that there was almost no crime among the Baptist teenagers: no hooliganism, no theft, no rape, no murder, nothing. Well, here is one instance where you can say: "We, the Baptists, give this country a moral youth."'

As one can imagine, I was very surprised that this man volunteered to give me such advice. It certainly triggered a lot of thinking, and the end result was that, in August that year, I went up to the Carpathian Mountains and I wrote what came to be known as *The Christian Manifesto*. My title for it was: *The Place of a Christian in the Socialist Society*.

By that time, the communists had been in power for almost 30 years. It was clear that they had failed to create that society of justice, equality, brotherhood and plenty which they had promised when they took power. Why the failure of such a great promise? My impression at that time was that socialism, as an economic and social type of organisation, was the ideal for mankind. The only trouble was in man, in the individual who was called to make that system function. As a Christian who believed in the corrupt nature of every man and in the power of Jesus Christ to bring about a radical transformation of that nature, I wanted to shout to the Marxists and to tell them: Here is the solution to your problem: let Christ loose in the system and let Him produce the new man needed by socialism, and the system will work.

On the 28th day of August, 1974, I sent a copy of my paper to Mr Nicolae Ceausescu, the president of

10

Romania. His reaction: on 4 October, he sent seven policemen to our house, and they searched it from six in the morning until two in the afternoon. They confiscated all my library and all our personal notes and letters, and they charged me with 'Propaganda which endangers the security of the State'.

I was placed under house arrest, and for six months I had to be available for interrogation. They would call me on the telephone, usually at eight in the morning, and sometimes the interrogation would be eight or ten hours per day. Eventually, as a result of strong protests in the West, President Ceausescu decided it would be too detrimental to his interests abroad to put me in prison, and they dropped the charge and set me free.

A year later, a group of European evangelical theologians met in Brussels. They sent a telegram to President Ceausescu about my library. Exactly two weeks after they sent the telegram, I was called to the police station and they returned all my books to me.

When Keston College received my manuscript in the autumn of 1974, they made the suggestion that I work a little more on it, give it a scientific apparatus of quotations, facts, references, and make it an academic paper. When my good friend Alan Scarfe brought me this message, I replied, 'Alan, when Karl Marx wrote his *Communist Manifesto*, a direct message to the masses, with no quotes or figures, but incendiary ideas, he kindled Europe with it. Then he went into the library and got facts and figures and quotes, and he made it into *Das Kapital*, a heavy work very few people dare approach and read. I want my paper to be readable like the *Communist Manifesto*, not heavy and unreadable like *Das Kapital*.' Then Alan said, 'Well, then, we should call your paper *The Christian Manifesto*.' And this is how it got the new title.

Now that it is to be reprinted, I have a very strong reservation. As I said above, my basic premise in this paper was that socialism as a system was good; the only problem was that corrupt people make it a corrupt system, and so the solution to make it work was to have people transformed through the power of Jesus Christ. Since then, I have given a lot of time to research and thought about it. I have come to see that it is socialism, as a system, which inevitably and naturally produces the centralised dictatorship, the police surveillance and oppression of the people, the total control exercised over everything and everybody in the system, the total regimentation of the society, and the total enslavement of the individual to the interests of the State.

The above are not the product of certain wicked leaders in the socialist countries. They are the natural outcome of a system which demands central planning, central enforcement of the plan, central control of everyone, and the transformation of those who carry out the plan into robots who do everything according to the plan.

Of course, it would take a whole book to show how

socialism inevitably produces all these phenomena which cause it to be such an undesirable system that it drives people away, rather than attracts. The fact that the Iron Curtain and the Bamboo Curtain are meant to keep people in, and the fact that the majority of refugees in the world today are people who run away from socialism represent the most obvious evidence of the failure of socialism. It is clear that after 70 years of Marxist experimentation, there is no country based on Marxist principles which is economically successful, and whose general situation is so greatly improved that the rest of mankind want to go and live there.

As one approaches my *Christian Manifesto*, one should be aware, then, that my view of socialism, as a system, has radically changed. Why I consider this paper still worth reading is because of its analysis of the failure of Marxism to produce the new man it is supposed to produce, and for the Christian message that only Jesus Christ is able to change and re-create the human person completely.

Joseph Ton
Wheaton, IL USA
February 1985

Marxism: The Faded Dream

For the past ten years the idea has been spreading in the West that the Christian has no place in the Socialist State. This is perilous both for the State and for Christian teaching. Those who propagate this view claim that genuine Christians are obliged to carry out their activities 'underground'. Their attitude is one of hostility towards the socialist system.

These claims have increased to the point that every Christian Church which functions in socialist countries 'with the approval of the Communists' is an apostate church. Every pastor who serves in such a church is a traitor. Only those churches which exist underground and pursue clandestine activities constitute the true church. The press propaganda of such groups tells tourists who visit socialist countries not to be impressed or enchanted by the over-flowing churches they will be shown. These are 'shop windows' arranged by the Communists to throw star dust in the eyes of the credulous, uninformed Western visitors.

This idea has taken deep root in many minds. A Czechoslovakian scientific researcher was invited to speak to Christian students at Oxford University in

1969. The first student question was this: 'First of all, please tell us whether you are a member of an "underground" or an "official" church?' When he replied that there were no 'underground' churches in his country, the students refused to listen any further. As far as they were concerned, this man was not a true Christian.

The power of this idea in the West is evident from an interview between a Dutch Christian reporter and President Ceausescu of Romania, given in the spring of 1973, when one of the questions asked was, 'What place has the Church in a Socialist State?'

Here lies a central problem for academic and political discussion: namely, the place of the Christian in socialism. The discussion is not closed nor the problem resolved by a simple demonstration that Romania's Constitution accords the right of religious practice to its citizens, and that in fact 14 denominations exist which function within the law. It is more complicated than that. It involves not only law, but also ideological and political questions. Consequently, there needs to be a theoretical debate which outlines all the ideological and political aspects which religion, and in particular Christianity hold in the Socialist State.

The purpose of this paper is to sketch out these aspects and to initiate a new dialogue on this whole subject.

Has the Christian any place in the Socialist State?

While in Oxford, as well as in other English Universities, I became involved in many discussions with students on the situation of religion and believers in socialist countries.

Such discussions usually opened with a question about the authenticity of information concerning the persecution and torture of believers in Socialist States. Inevitably they led to this fundamental question: 'Has the Christian any place in the Socialist State? Are Christians merely tolerated until they eventually disappear, the State doing all it can to aid the process? Or are they accepted in society as CHRISTIANS, with full rights in every sphere of social life, and are they engaged as such in the construction of socialist society?'

On one such occasion, an Oxford student put the following extremely logical and fundamental question, which to my amazement had not been asked before: 'I don't understand why Marxism is against religion. After all, what has Marxism to do with religion?' That question put me on the spot and I did not know how to answer it. But the essential importance of the question was such that I determined to do everything possible to find the answer. It was obvious that a dialogue on this general theme of the place of a Christian in Socialism must begin from this question, and that the resolution of the subject as a whole depends on the answer given to it.

Why is Marxism against religion?

It is known that Marx, Lenin and Stalin were all deeply interested in religion in their youth. They studied it seriously and wrote about it sympathetically. What caused all these men to turn against religion, and to find it imperative to fight for religion's destruction, its removal from men's thoughts and lives? In Oxford I found a pamphlet by the same author who had launched the theory of 'underground' churches in Socialist countries. In the pamphlet he attempts an explanation of the aversion of Marxist-Leninists for religion in terms of certain traumatic experiences which they had had with the Church of Christianity in general. Marx suffered together with his father, a Jew who became a Christian to help his chances of promotion in the administrative machine of anti-Semitic Germany. Lenin, if I remember correctly, suffered the shock of the church's pettiness on the occasion of his brother's execution. Stalin was disillusioned in a theological seminary at Tbilisi where he was once a student. These traumatic experiences made them enemies of religion in general. This attributing of a vast social phenomenon to the unfortunate experiences of a handful of people, even though they were the creators of Marxism-Leninism, seems to be inadequate.

Many years of Marxist studies at school and university, and ten years of further Marxist indoctrination while I was a teacher in the country, have taught me that an idea cannot take root and become a phenomenon of the masses unless it meets with favourable social and political conditions.

Therefore, applying Marxist thought to the interpretation of an aspect of Marxism, I posed this pertinent question to myself. What special historical conditions persuaded the teachers of Marxism-Leninism to consider the religious problem so important that they gave a good part of their time to it? What particularly were they pursuing in their fight against idealism in general and against Christianity in particular? There must have been specific social and political conditions which determined this course of action. Whatever the personal experiences of Marx or Lenin may have been, these would have remained personal. They would not normally have been transformed into a mass movement.

Anyone who understands the historical conditions of the last century will have an obvious answer to these questions. Marx lived much of his life in England where, at that time, almost 65% of the population attended church every Sunday. England was a country where the majority of people were practising Christians, among whom were a major proportion of the working classes. In England Marx discovered the mechanism of capitalist exploitation and worked out the pattern of revolution which would end this exploitation. He believed that the proletarian revolution must be realised in the country which had at that time the most developed industry and the largest number of the proletariat. It was at this very point that the projected revolution collided with the religious world outlook.

When the working class believe in a better life in heaven and trust in a God who punishes violence, there can be no revolution. A man who believes in a better life beyond the grave will not risk eternity by venturing into a war for happiness in this ephemeral life, particularly if victory is uncertain. The person who believes that God punishes the murderer will never raise his hand against his exploiters. He will leave vengeance and his liberation from misery to God, regardless of whether these things happen now or in eternity. To the creators of Marxism-Leninism religion was an obstacle on the road to revolution, and this, above all else, led the Marxist teachers to fight against idealism in general and Christianity in particular.

Their main problem was this: for a man to be persuaded to take up arms in protest against 'the crude and unjust system' he had first to arrive at two psychological states. First, he needed to be a desperate man, a man without any hope in an afterlife, who had reached the conclusion that the present is his only chance. Secondly, he had to be a man without scruples, who 'knows' that God does not exist to punish (or reward) him and who consequently is not troubled by his conscience when faced with the question of armed violence against those who withhold material goods. Marxism-Leninism believed that only atheism could produce such a man.

In general, they were convinced that a special ideology will produce a certain character in man, and this fundamental and vitally important conviction was significant for the future of Socialism. They understood that atheistic ideology would inevitably produce a desperate, unscrupulous man, capable of carrying through a bloody revolution.

The revolution's realisation demanded the creation of such a character, and it was this which led the Marxist teachers to launch their attack against religion by indoctrinating the working classes with atheistic ideology, action which they called 'the ideological preparation for revolution'. Clearly, the simple traumatic experience of religion by individuals did not produce a phenomenon of mass proportions. The simple discovery by Marx, Engels or Lenin, that the Bible was not true—supposing that they discovered that it was not true—would not have made them fight for its defeat, squandering precious revolutionary time on a discussion which would have been purely academic for them. It was their sincere, incensed desire to rid the working masses of exploitation which made them begin this. The necessity of such a special type of revolutionary man made them attack the Christian faith, regardless of the truth or falsehood of Christianity.

Here is the answer to the question, 'Why is Marxism against religion?' But to what extent does it help us to understand the problems of the place of the Christian in Socialism? We will understand this better if we analyse the consequences for Socialism of its campaign against idealism and Christianity, which was initiated before the revolution and was continued by virtue of inertia, after the success of the revolution.

The new man

There is an observation of first importance which must be made now. The desperate and unscrupulous man through whom the revolution had to be realised was not foreseen by the Marxist-Leninist teachers as an essential ingredient of the communist society which was meant to be established as a result of the revolution. On the contrary, in regard to that society they introduced a new special concept, that of the 'new man'.

The 'new man' has two major attributes. First, that man in socialism should not be alienated from the means of production. All means of production will be the property of everyone. Therefore, man will yield all his energies, freely, to the process of producing material goods for society as a whole, and by this he will discover fulfilment in the creative process. Secondly, this man, freed from corruption by the strength of the socialist system, will handle the goods honestly and will distribute them freely, taking only as much as he needs so that enough will remain for all his kinsmen. He will be a man who will yield all his forces freely for others, a totally committed altruist. This was the dream that Marxist-Leninist teachers had of the 'new man' in socialism, and without whom they clearly demonstrated that communism could not be realised. They were convinced that a radical and essential change of man's character would happen automatically, once the economic, political and social systems were altered.

Today, many years after the revolution has passed, it is clear that socialist man's character has not changed. He has remained as he was in the capitalist society, an egoist, full of vice and devoid of uprightness. It follows that the creation of the 'new man' still remains today a 'burden' to be realised, the fulfilment of which is for ever encountering obstacles.

Why is it that this 'new man' refuses to appear in conformity to all the visions and expectations? (Not to be misunderstood, I must make it clear that we are not suggesting that there are no men in today's

Socialist society who are altruistic, correct, or of a noble character – far from it, but we are referring to the 'new man' as a general phenomenon of the masses, which is far from happening.)

The present impasse, from a historical point of view, has been caused by the materialistic concept of man. The general materialistic world outlook is the very fact which maintains and will perpetuate the situation in which 'new man' as a mass phenomenon will not be able to appear.

An examination of the materialistic concept of man reveals the type of social-political being produced by this concept. Marxist teachers considered man's character to be the product of his environment. The social systems of serfdom, feudalism, and capitalism were corrupt, based on the exploitation of man. Their social characteristics were theft, violence and dishonesty. No man shaped within these systems could escape, and of necessity acquired a vicious character, similar to the system which produced him. Subsequently, since a man is only the product of his environment, one needs only to create a social system founded on justice and honour to produce a man of noble character. A just system will produce an honest, upright man. Lenin, thinking along these lines, not long before the revolution wrote that Marxists did not consider it necessary to preach morality to the working classes. The bourgeois did this with the intention of keeping the workers in subjection. Marxists have a better way.

They will change the social order, and this in its turn will produce a new type of man.

There are indications that very soon after the 1917 revolution, Lenin realised that the hope in the spontaneous appearance of the new man in socialism was not being fulfilled. In spite of changing the social-political system, man's character did not change. On the contrary, the problem of corruption and dishonesty in the socialist administration became one of the most serious deficiencies of the system.

There is documentation in the West that in about 1921, when this mistake about the expected spontaneous appearance of the new character of socialist man was realised and the problem of how to change man's character reached an acute pitch, Lenin heard of Pavlov's experiments with dogs' conditioned reflexes and summoned him to the Kremlin. He asked whether it was possible to apply these experiments to men, so that a new man could be produced with a new behaviour in society. Pavlov, who believed men were merely advanced animals, replied positively. Lenin asked Pavlov to write down his method for creating in the whole of human society a new type of character with conditioned reflexes. Pavlov was retained for three months at the Kremlin where he wrote a 400-page paper. This has never been removed from the Kremlin, but stands behind the vast campaign for the reform of soviet society in the decades before

1940. All that happened in those years was with the purpose of conditioning man, in the hope that the new man, who otherwise was refusing to appear, might be achieved.

Man is not a mere animal, however, and no matter how much conditioning he undergoes, he refuses to conform. Sooner or later he will reassert himself as man and reject the plans of those who treated him like a dog. Pavlovianism, applied to a human society in the interest of producing the new man essential to socialist and communist society, achieved nothing but immense suffering and terrible tragedy for millions of people.

The materialist concept of man, as a simple product of a specific medium, led to a socio-political mistake. Instead of bringing joy to society it brought terror and horror. This concept of man does not help. On the contrary, it hinders the process of creating a new man.

Marxist-Leninist teachers believed that a certain ideology was going to lead to a certain attitude towards life and society, and that the materialist, atheist ideology would lead to desperation and an armed conflict for a better life. Marx, Engels and Lenin preached atheism merely to create despair in man, and to drive him to any lengths to obtain a larger share of the world's goods. Their philosophical materialism had nothing to do with the truth or falsehood of religion. Atheism, as they saw it, did not have within its scope the establishment or triumph of academic truth. It pursued the creation of a man capable of revolution. But such a man was only necessary for the short period of the revolution. After the revolution succeeded it was hoped that man would be totally seeking the common good, a man of the highest, most noble, moral character.

Here we face a contradiction in Marxist thought. Before the revolution a specific *ideology* was proclaimed which would produce a particular attitude in man. A short time after the revolution it was believed that the new economic, social and political *system* would produce a new attitude, a new character in man. This failure to produce a new man raises a fundamental question. What produces the character of man, social order or ideology? Is the character of man an automatic product of social forces, or is character shaped by the world outlook which inspires a man?

We believe that the evolution of events in so many countries this century demonstrates beyond doubt that ideology, or the way men conceive or understand the world, and the life, shapes and forms one's character. As a sufficient proof of this, take an example outside socialism, the monstrosities produced by Hitler's ideology.

Assuming this, we must ask an important question: 'Since a particular ideology produces a particular character, and atheism produces a character which is not essential to a victorious socialism, but on the contrary hinders it, why do we

29

continue to spread an ideology which works against socialism?' That is to say, why continue, after the revolution, to propagate the materialistic and atheistic concept of life which produces unscrupulous and desperate men? Our aim is by detailed demonstration to establish that the materialist or the atheist view of life hinders the appearance, the formation of the new man on a mass scale in our socialist society.

Education to produce the new man

In Romania there is wide acceptance of the view that education is the determining factor in the formation of character. It was the task of the schools to produce the new man needed by the Socialist State. I remember how in the '60s, when I was a teacher, each autumn, in his remarks to the teaching staff, our local Communist party leader impressed upon us our primary responsibility to produce the new man. This idea was boringly repeated time and time again. Why could the school not succeed in rising to the task assigned by the Party?

I will try to answer this by recalling an incident from my own teaching career. I was a teacher in a Cluj High School, and one autumn was elected president of the school's Committee of Directors. It was my job to coordinate all the school's educational activities. The aim of the whole process was to create the new man. While reflecting on my task I constantly encountered an obstacle in my way. I went to the Communist Party Secretary of the school, a young physics teacher, to discuss the problem and to seek his advice. I said to him:

'The teachers, like you, of physics, chemistry and natural science, go into the classrooms and give the pupils a scientific outlook on life. You teach them that the world is merely matter in infinite motion. Life is a form of existence of this matter, which has appeared through the chance interplay of infinite combinations of matter, and man is the most complex organised form of these chance combinations. According to you the whole complex of plant, animal and human life is governed by Darwinian laws of adaptation and the survival of the most adaptable individuals and species. There is no other life than this one. The end of this life is the end of man's only chance. There is no afterlife where another opportunity exists. There is no God who will on the one hand reward self-sacrifice, or on the other punish egoism or rapacity. After all this has been said to the students, you send me in to teach them that they ought to be noble and honourable men and women. They must expend all their energies on doing good for the benefit of society, even to the point of self-sacrifice. They must be courteous, tell only the truth and live a morally pure life.

'When the thoughtful students hear my words, they say, "But, teacher, in a purely material world, where life is governed by Darwinian laws, and where only he who hurries and grabs for himself possesses anything, why must we be altruistic, honest and everything else you tell us?"

'You see my problem. These boys and girls are at the age of great vision and aspiration. Their ideals about nobility of character are being formed. I want to make them good men, but I lack one thing – a motivation for goodness and nobility of character. Why should anyone be self-denying, courteous or honest? If I could put reasonable motives to them for being men of character, I could make them of the finest nobility. Tell me, in a purely materialistic world where life is the product of a game of chance and where man's single chance is here and now, and consequently he who has, is the strongest one who knows how to seize things for himself, what motive can we offer them to live lives of usefulness to others, or even self-sacrifice?'

I will never forget that moment! The young physics teacher took a long look at me, smiled, and said, 'Friend, do you want me to be honest with you?' 'Of course,' I replied, 'that's why I came, so we could talk honestly.' 'Well,' he went on, 'I do not see, personally, why I should be good and honest. I know that if I don't pull some strings, or stab someone in the back, I will not advance or succeed in life. And this is everything for me.'

Our conversation ended there, and it illustrates perfectly the position in which any atheistically-based school finds itself when it is a matter of meeting the required task of producing the new man in socialism.

Recently, I have asked many Marxist ideologists how Marxist philosophy endeavours to promote morality and nobility of character. They replied that the only way of inspiring the giving of self for others is to claim that the pursuit of the common good means the realisation of personal good. However, they pointed out that this motivation fails when an individual realises that this common good is only slowly achieved, is a process that may last for generations, and that by using the various levers and means available to him he can have the goods now, ahead of the majority. Once a person knows this, there is no moral principle preventing him using every means for personal advantage, even if it is detrimental to society.

The Socialist society finds itself in a paradoxical situation. It desires a new man of noble character, but it propagates an ideology which cannot offer men any assistance or inspiration for ennobling his character. Furthermore, it pushes men towards desperate and dishonest action, to a life-style totally dominated by egoistic purposes.

The situation protests loudly, Gentlemen, don't you understand that the spreading of atheistic, materialistic ideology works against the interests of the society you want to build? Stop creating unscrupulous, desperate men, for socialist society has no need of such a thing.

We have established above that Marx, Engels and Lenin came to understand that a specific ideology produces a specific type of man with certain dominant impulses and a certain norm of behaviour. In addition, we saw that a materialistic, atheistic concept of life and the world leads a man to the point of desperation and creates a desire in him to get as much as he can for himself by any means. We have also noticed that the academic question of the right or the wrong of a particular ideology was of no relevance to them. They were more interested to know which ideology would reduce the working classes to such a state of agitation that they would be ready to take up arms, overthrow capitalism and set up socialism.

It was for this reason and with this objective in mind that they began to spread the materialistic, atheistic concept of life. Furthermore, we have seen that after the realisation of the revolution, i.e. in socialism, society had no further need of an atmosphere which drove men to revolution. Now society needed a settled man, integrated into the world, society and himself, who was ready to offer all his energies for the sake of the common good.

Consequently, to continue promoting an ideology which was intended to produce a man desperate to the point of revolution was sheer folly.

The Creative Force

The question which logically follows is this: 'If Marxist-Leninist teachers understood that ideology makes the man, which ideology is capable of producing the new man, of high aspiration and noble character, who will sacrifice himself for the common good and be absolutely upright in his social behaviour?' The only answer is the ideology of the one who possessed the most noble character of all, Jesus Christ, who sacrificed himself for the good of His fellow men. His character, His self-sacrifice on Calvary and His teaching how a man should live, expressed principally in the Sermon on the Mount, Matthew chapters 5–7, have for almost 2,000 years not ceased to produce the finest men who ever walked the earth.

It is well known that great socialists from the past century drank from this spring. They acknowledged Jesus Christ as their most outstanding inspirer. They even considered Him the first socialist or communist in history. It is certain that the first community of Christ's disciples and followers formed in Jerusalem was organised on a communist basis. They put into practice the spirit of His teaching. The rich sold their goods and put them at the disposal of the Apostles, so that they could be used for the sustaining of the entire community. In Acts 2:44–45 the Jerusalem society is described. Wherever the spirit of Christ's teaching was accepted and assimilated in its totality, the result was a noble life put to the service of the common good, even at the cost of self-sacrifice.

The important feature is not just the teaching of Jesus Christ, but His person, life and death on Calvary. When an individual accepts these as having been given for him, there is a radical fundamental transformation of the individual's essential being. The most desperate drunkard experiences a genuine aversion to alcohol and becomes completely teetotal. Adulterers abandon their life of debauchery and become family men. Those weak in character grow in strength and integrity. Today, it is common knowledge that some young people addicted to drugs are unable to escape despite medical help. Yet, if they are converted, if they pass through an experience of being transformed in being and character by accepting Jesus into their lives, they completely escape its fatal influence.

The Apostle Paul was the first to remark on the transforming effect of Christ's sacrifice on behalf of mankind. It became a central topic of his sermons. He first coined the concept of 'the new man'. He began by making the universal declaration, 'If anyone is in Christ, he is a new creation.'

(2 Corinthians 5:17.) Acceptance of Christ and union with Him produces such fundamental changes in man that it is possible to speak of man as a new creation. Later, Paul introduced the precise term 'the new man' in his written addresses to some who were united to Christ in this way. He was showing them the mode of their life as it should be in Christ. See Ephesians 4:22–24; Romans 13:12–14; Colossians 3:9–14.

Paul's concept of the new man was not an innovation. He was developing an idea enunciated by Christ Himself. Christ demonstrated that human beings were in need of a radical transformation, which He called 'the new birth'. For example, in conversation with Nicodemus, the aged scholar, Jesus said, 'If a man is not born again he cannot enter the Kingdom of God' (John 3:3). The Apostle John explained this further when he wrote, 'Jesus came to his own and his own would not receive him, but to all who did receive him he gave the right to become the children of God; that is to all who believe, who were born not of blood, nor of the will of the flesh, nor of the will of man, but of God.' (John 1:12.)

The Bible sets out the kernel of man's problem in this way. Man's character is corrupt, his nature is so marred that no superficial measure can restore it. According to Jesus' graphic description, just as a wild tree cannot produce good fruit, so man in his natural state is incapable of leading a moral life. A tree must be grafted to produce good fruit, and a man requires the radical transformation of the new birth, or a recreation. This can only be achieved through union with Christ, by trust in His divinity, and a personal acceptance of Him. Christ is par excellence, the New Man. He is the prototype of the New Humanity, the originator of a new kind of man, born of God, and destined to reign eternally with Him. He who receives Christ into his life is 'clothed in Christ', or 'clothed in the New Man'. He becomes a new man, a new creation, and from that moment forward his life is a new one, lived after Christ's pattern.

What does science say to all this? It is not unscientific to return to religion in the twentieth century? In answering this objection we shall not attempt to prove the scientific truth of Christianity. We could give a long list of contemporary books by famous authors who do just that. Equally, we could list books which attack Christianity. This discussion of the scientific truth or falsehood of the Faith has been going on for hundreds of years and will continue for many more.

We will rather respond by quoting the testimonies of men who believe and whose lives have been changed and heightened by a living faith in Christ. We can cite hundreds of modern scholars, including creators of modern scientific theories and winners of the Nobel Prize, who testify not only that belief in Christ does not prevent them thinking scientifically, but that it has actually helped, by giving sense, purpose and value to their life and work.

Religious experience of Christ cannot be denied by those who do not believe and have not had the experience, for they have no means of appreciating it. One modern researcher explained it thus: If religion is in essence part of a man's inner life, it follows that it cannot be assessed except from within. Without a doubt, this can only be done by that man in whose inner knowledge religious experience has a place. An unbeliever who attempts to speak about religion is in the same position as a blind man trying to describe colour, or a deaf man talking about a wonderful piece of music.

Far from denying the value of religion, modern science shows its indispensable character for a wholly integrated human personality. One of the major categories of modern science is that of 'structure'. Structuralism is a current theme in every science. Structures, basic patterns are being sought everywhere, in mathematics, chemistry, philology, etc. It is interesting that those who study human societies from a variety of angles tell us that man is born with certain inherent structures. Whether the structures are of language, thought or emotions, all wait to be fulfilled, satisfied and lived out. Otherwise, if one or other of them is unfulfilled, the human personality seems diminished, impoverished, unrealised.

On these lines, some leading scholars of world

renown tell us that one of man's inherent structures is religion, a structure which finds expression in the fact that men in every age and civilisation have felt the strong need of a Being which is beyond and the imperative desire to communicate with Someone in the Great Beyond, whom they have never seen but whose existence they intuitively perceive. This structure, of religion, has become an object of scientific investigation.

At Oxford in 1968, a study group under the leadership of no less a person than a former President of the British Royal Academy, Sir Alistair Hardy, began an examination of religious structures in a scientific way. It is essential to remember that the religious life is a part of man's structure, without which man will have a permanent sense of incompleteness, a feeling of inner emptiness, a desire for an indefinable something, which in the end leads a man to believe he is unfulfilled, his destiny not accomplished.

If socialism seeks the complete fulfilment of human personality, and this is its declared intention, then it must take note of the religious dimensions of man which seek to be realised. Augustine recognised this dimension, structure or capacity for the religious life when he wrote so vividly, 'Our souls are made for Thee, O God, and they find no rest until they rest in Thee.'

C. J. Jung in our own day, towards the end of a lifetime devoted to psychiatry, declared that he had found in man what he called the 'pattern of God'. The conclusion which Jung, a master of modern psychiatry, drew about the necessity of religion for individuals was this: 'During the past thirty years, men from every civilised country in the world have come to me for consultation. Among all my mature patients there was not one whose problem did not spring from a lack of religious world outlook. I can assure you that each of them had become ill because they had not that which only a living religion gives to a man, and not one of them will recover fully, unless he regains the religious view of life.'

More than this, religion is not only vital for an individual, it is equally essential for social survival. Professor Evans-Pritchard, of the Anthropology School in Oxford University, points out that 'the functioning of religion is essential for the survival of the human race'. Proof lies in the fact that societies have existed without science or philosophy, but there has never been a human society without religion. Religion, as a permanent factor throughout human history, is an integral part of our human structure.

Religion, instead of harming man, as those who oppose and seek to defend man from it maintain, is structurally and vitally necessary. It is, in fact, the dimension which raises men above the animal world, the agent which lifts a man into the Divine World.

An adulterated Christianity

Why has Christianity in its 2,000 years of existence not achieved the ideal Christian society? How is it that in the name of religion, over the years, so many atrocities have been committed? An answer to these questions will be found in a historical look at Christianity. In the first centuries after Christ, Christianity was still lively, following the original teaching of its founder, Jesus Christ, and His Apostles, and no additions were made from Greek philosophy and pagan superstitions. The church was not yet an institution and it produced wonderful men and marvellous Christian communities. As time passed, Christianity's original source was neglected, and preference was given to later teachers influenced by neo-Platonism and other thought-forms foreign to the Gospel. These were known as the Holy Fathers and their writings were later collectively called the Holy Tradition.

Later, in the fourth century, Christianity was adopted for political reasons as the state religion of the Roman Empire and the church became a political force. Less emphasis was put on the power of Christ to change the individual and society, and more was placed on the power of the church to decide the fate of men's souls. The idea was introduced that the church had power to forgive sins, to release men from sin, to save them and to ~~ them of a place in heaven. The practice introduced at that time is well known. The individual could lead any sort of life as long as he came to the priest occasionally to confess and be absolved from his sins. Once more he would commit the same misdeeds, then call on the priest again for absolution! This process continued till at his death-bed the priest absolved him of all his sins and thus opened the way to heaven for him.

The idea was prevalent that the Church could intervene on someone's behalf after death, and if relatives paid the required 'fee', sins could be forgiven post mortem, the soul being transferred from a state of damnation to happiness. This perversion took its worst form when the Catholic Church commercialised the forgiveness of sins by the sale of indulgences.

This form of Christianity had two significant consequences for our thesis. Firstly, it concentrated the whole of religious life within the hands of the church's priests. These men knew the magic formula to bind and release, they mediated between man and God, and, in a word, they enjoyed a monopoly of the spiritual world. Individuals were not encouraged either to read religious literature for themselves, or to cultivate a personal spiritual life. On the contrary, people were driven away, isolated, from them. Secondly, the individual, aware that the priest could release him from sin's consequences, was in no way stimulated to lead a moral life. The situation encouraged a life free from restraint or care. We can understand why a nationalised, institutionalised religion lost the revolutionary power which had been able to transform individuals and society.

Protestantism came to restore original Christianity precisely at these sore points. Firstly, it rejected every later addition to the faith, i.e. the 'Holy Tradition', and called Christianity back to its source, the Bible. Secondly, it spurned as unbiblical and unchristian the idea that the priest could be a mediator between man and God, on the basis that Scripture said, 'there is one mediator between God and men, the man Christ Jesus,' (1 Timothy 2:5). The individual was left alone before God. Subsequent consequences of the reformation were of profound importance for the development of human individuality.

First it put the Bible into man's hands, where he could read it for himself and thus develop his own spiritual life. He no longer had the consolation that someone else, namely the Church, would look after his soul. Secondly, being brought face to face with God, the individual became responsible. He now knew the seriousness of sin to God, that the death of Christ was necessary for forgiveness, and that his whole life was passing in review before God to whom he must answer at the last day for his mode of living. The individual's direct, personal contact with ᵗhrough his union with Christ, that is with ˡᶜ-sacrifice and resurrected personality, had ᵐing effects. When this experience became general, on a national scale, the improvement that society in some countries experienced was immense. Sweden, Norway, Denmark and England, for instance, where Protestantism had a nation-wide impact, became proverbial for the honesty among their citizens and the integrity of their administrative apparatus. All that was achieved positively in these countries was realised under the influence of Protestant Christianity, which demonstrated its power to revolutionise and transform men and society. Also, we must forcibly underline that these countries are alone in realising a society which almost met the ideal of integrity, honesty and moral purity. No other form of Christianity or other religion has ever achieved anything similar.

Someone will object that what happened in these countries during the last century and beginning of this one has been destroyed today. It is well known that the greatest debauchery and most promiscuity takes place in Scandinavia today. But does the fact that high moral attainment has not actually lasted weaken our argument? No, not at all. A proper understanding of the process of moral decline in these lands will confirm and strengthen our thesis.

Darwinism and Liberal Theology

The decline and later complete abandonment of religion in Protestant countries originates from the time of Charles Darwin. Until then creation theory had an unassailable position. No alternative theory of origins existed. Scientists were unable to show how such a complex organisation as the world could happen of its own accord. However, Darwin offered them a fascinating and attractive theory, extremely logical and apparently impossible to combat. It concerned the way in which beings had developed on earth from the most simple organisms to the most complex: the theory of evolution.

The theory won over the scientific world quickly and almost totally. It offered an entirely fresh explanation of origins and a new way of looking at life and the world we live in. The theological world felt the shaking impact of this new scientific weapon immediately. Some people, aware of its destructive character with regard to man's faith, reacted with a violence which was near to panic. Their opposition was ineffective, because they lacked any equivalent logically convincing argument. Other theologians, mainly the most learned and important men, accepted the new theory as inevitable and scientifically accurate. It is from this stage that we can trace the falling away. These theologians were the scholastic authorities, and they began to re-interpret the Bible and to claim that it had no pretensions to be scientific or to offer an explanation of the material world. Biblical writers, they said, belonged to a pre-scientific era, and they mirrored their own concepts of the world. The Bible does not contain explanations of the scientific material world, but rather advice of a purely spiritual kind. Where science bring us an explanation of the world which differs from the Bible, we must bear in mind the naiveté of the biblical authors and accept the explanation offered by science.

This appeared very reasonable. Theologians did not intend to destroy the Bible or faith. Despite the naiveté they attributed to biblical writers, they nevertheless found sufficient material with spiritual value in it for the Bible to hold some place in their thinking. But, for the great mass of believers the theologians' attitude had catastrophic effects. In the course of one generation the percentage of regular church attendance in England fell from 65% to 10%. In Sweden, where the percentage was higher than in Britain, less than 5% of the population now frequent church. Only in America did the percentage remain constant around 50%, but this was due to the strong fight of the Fundamentalists against the theory of evolution.

Before turning to the scientific truth or falsehood of the evolutionary theory, its disastrous effect on the morality of the protestant countries must be noted. Simultaneous with a decline of the evangelical faith was an abandonment of any kind of moral standard. Society in these lands is at present experiencing a nightmare of debauchery and an invasion of pornography unknown in Europe since the decline of the Roman Empire.

What is proved beyond doubt is that reformation Christianity succeeded in an unprecedented manner to create a moral man and a pure society, but the abandonment of the faith resulted in the moral decline of these societies.

One hundred years after Darwin, the scientific world is undergoing a new revolution. Geological, zoological, biological and especially genetic research are undermining, not confirming, the evolutionary theory. Even though some academics are still bound by this theory, since they have no valid alternative yet, except creationism which they regard as unscientific, many great and celebrated scholars recognise that the evolutionary theory is outdated. It can explain neither the appearance of the world, the origin of life, animal species, nor man.

This is not the place to pursue further such a hotly contested issue. All we must underline is that scholars are no longer as sure as once they were. Today, the relativity theory is not only a physics theory, but it also expresses a general attitude towards science. No longer can even convinced materialists allow only one theory of the world's origin and development.

In contrast to the self-assured arrogance of the past, the Western Universities are marked by the remarkable phenomenon of scientific modesty, and scientists no longer rush to draw up hasty generalisations. Discoveries today follow each other with such rapidity that theories are constantly being revised and new ones substituted in a decade at the most. This makes scientists appreciate the relativity of all scientific explanations. The discovery of other physical worlds around us with other laws and forms of existence, together with the new science of para-psychology, makes scholars very cautious about claims that our material world is the only one which exists.

It is further agreed that materialism has created an immense spiritual vacuum. As long as the scientific world was shielded with a conviction of absolute knowledge, the emptiness was not felt. But now the scholars are not sure any more. And to the scientific uncertainty the humanist philosophy adds the anguish of the lack of purpose in life. The emptiness is felt mainly in moments of tragedy when science can no longer give a confident answer. Man's soul can never be satisfied with purely material and cultural goods. Man thirsts for a spiritual world and cannot be satisfied with less than a living contact with it. Spiritual hunger, aspirations after the tran-scendent, and an avid seeking of religious experience is the new, dominant characteristic of the younger generation in the West and the East, both in capital-ist and socialist societies.

If today there are fundamental revisions being carried out in science, the same is happening in theology. It is now accepted that theologians rushed ahead too hastily in their attempts to adapt the Bible to Darwinian theology. The overwhelming majority of places in the Bible which were contested by science have since proved capable of resisting attack. The truth of the Bible has been proved.

The theologians who sought to shape the Bible to evolutionary thought and science in general, which changes its position from one decade to another, made a very expensive mistake. Firstly, they denied biblical truth for a love of so-called science. Secondly, by this denial they undermined the moral foundations of entire nations, destroying what had been a most wonderful achievement in modern history.

The role of the Christian in socialist society

This paper's aim is to establish the place in socialism of Christianity, especially of neo-protestantism. Have Baptists, Pentecostals, Brethren, any role as Christians in a socialist society? Is a Christian accepted as such by society? Will he be given the trust which will enable him to work in any employment at any level? If we stop at the question in its first form and seek a legal answer, we shall have to reply in the affirmative. The Constitution of Romania gives its citizens the right to assert and to practise a religious belief, and the 1948 Law of Cults legitimises some fourteen religious denominations, including those mentioned above.

If we asked the third form of the question in the

paragraph above, there could not be so confident an answer. Those who know the treatment which has been accorded to believers of the neo-protestant denominations would give a categorical no! Neo-protestant Christians in Romania are treated with great mistrust. Certain jobs are closed to them, as are certain levels of the social hierarchy. Pressure is mounted from all sides and they face exceptional discrimination. They cannot but feel that they are only tolerated by society, and we shall see that this is, in fact, their real situation, not only in Romania, but in every socialist state.

The discrepancy between the Constitution and what happens in practice can only be appreciated by understanding the socialist religious policy. Socialism set out with the hope that in a socialist system, religion would rapidly disappear, certainly within one generation. I remember how this was explained to us in the meetings for political indoctrination we had to attend in 1948–1949. Despite the popular, simplistic explanation given at that time, it laid down in essence the directives for the future. 'We know from history,' it was said, 'that persecution and martyrdom only kindle the flame of religious zeal and therefore we do not wish to repeat this mistake. We have a better method. We will leave the mature and old religious people to practise their beliefs, for once assimilated it is difficult to eradicate it from the mind. Rather, we will attend to the younger generation, isolating and protecting it from the influence of religious people. We have all the educational means in our hands, and we will raise up a new generation of atheists. And so religion will vanish away with the disappearance of the older generations of believers.'

The entire socialist policy on religion was centred on these lines. The confidence that religion would disappear in a generation in socialism was built on this theory. The first to have the courage to comment publicly on the theory was an East German theologian at a congress of the Lutheran Church held in the German Democratic Republic in 1972. Analysing the position of Christians as a result of this policy, he described it as one of 'toleration to vanishing point'. He said Christians had been granted a period of grace until they were snuffed out. Every regulation, prohibition and restriction of religious freedom of the churches, and particularly those imposed on the neo-protestants, for they manifest a more vigorous vitality and are in fact growing numerically, were imposed with the purpose of accelerating the hoped-for disappearance of religion in socialism.

Sociologists consider twenty-five years a generation. It is time we recognised that the hope of extinguishing religion has not been fulfilled. In the autumn of 1972, in the inaugural lecture of a course on atheism at the Philosophy Faculty of Bucharest, Lecturer Aurelian Tache, having outlined the old hope that religion would quickly vanish in socialism, showed that a statistical census taken in the area of Brasov to indicate the development of religion there over the past twenty-five years, found that religious sects (a derogatory term for neo-protestants) had grown by 300%. In practice, religion has not faded away in socialism, but there has been a deepening of religious phenomena. This is most blatantly obvious in the fifty years of Russian Socialism, despite the passing of two generations since the installation on the new social-political system.

In Romania today there are signs of great spiritual hunger among young people. They desire something transcendent. This phenomenon can be explained in sociological terms. In the years preceding socialism and in the short time after its establishment, people were told to renounce all expectations of an afterlife, on the basis that 'heaven is an illusion'. They were to concentrate on constructing a heaven on earth, here and now. In the enthusiasm and revolutionary romanticism of that time, large masses of men believed that paradise could be created on earth, and gave all their strength to its creation, abandoning in the process any notion of transcendency. They manifested a spirit of sacrifice for the sake of a new and happy life in this world. Years passed, and the earthly paradise was late in appearing. It is true that the standard of living rose, but it was too slow; much slower, in fact, than had been hoped for or promised. Then 'long term' plans were introduced and people began to appreciate that the prospect of a paradise on earth was extremely remote.

Afterwards, the gates were opened to foreign tourism, and contact with men from the West caused us to understand that the standard of living in capitalist countries was much higher than at home, and that many generations would have to pass before we could even reach the standard of the 'capitalist hell' let alone the realisation of our own communist paradise on earth.

At this moment man suffered a terrible shock, or rather an awakening to reality. He realised that he had abandoned a heavenly paradise for the earthly one. His love and his choice of material things had emptied him of spiritual life. Now, since the material paradise had become a long distance prospect, he remained totally empty, both inside and outside. He had hardly come to terms with the failure of his material plans when he recognised the full significance of his inner emptiness.

For balance we must emphasise the paradox that an exclusive desire for the attaining of material wealth, at the cost of sacrificing one's interest in the spiritual life, leads to the same end – the awareness of a vast inner emptiness. This also explains the reaction of young people in capitalist countries, which have achieved an abundance of material goods, who are disgruntled with the consumer society and are hungering after spiritual values.

Such developments in modern social life only

confirm that religion is an intimate part of man's makeup, and that whatever he is given in exchange for it will not satisfy or fulfil him unless he is put in a living contact with the spiritual reality for which he was created.

The fact that religion is not vanishing in socialism, but on the contrary gains strength, must cause, sooner or later, a revision and an alteration of the Communist Party's attitude towards this aspect of the individual and social life.

Recently I asked an outstanding Romanian Communist Party ideologist whether he would give me the philosophical reasons for fighting against religion. He replied that there were none, and could not see, logically, why so much energy was spent combatting it. From the philosophical point of view, men should be left to follow their religious beliefs. The present attitude on this, he said, was dictated by political reasoning, not philosophy.

The new man – only through Christ

We have already noted that the initial fight against Marxist religion by Marxist-Leninist teachers was dictated by political motives and was not in any way philosophical. One of the most fundamental purposes of this article has been to demonstrate that the primary purpose of their fight against religion, to produce the revolutionary man, was truly of a short duration. After the revolution had succeeded and the new socialist society was established, the fight against religion was harmful for socialism, and its continuance is a political mistake. Socialism is fighting against its own interests when it maintains the war against religion.

Socialism needs the new man, the moral man, as man himself needs the air he breathes. This new man cannot be created by slogans or by moral codes of behaviour. Laws will never assist a man to become a moral being. Paul understood this when he wrote that the law kills but the Spirit gives life. Only the spirit of Christ can revolutionise a man, transform him, and make him a new kind of person. Socialism needs the Spirit of Christ if it is to produce the new man. Roger Garaudy, in *Socialism at the Crossroads*, indicates clearly that socialism has faltered in its attempt to transform men and produce the new man. Che Guevara, that passionate revolutionary, said, 'If socialism does not mean the transformation of man's character, it does not interest me.' Socialism has tried many recipes to this end. Why does it see Christ as the enemy of this society, when He is its only chance?

This paper began by stating that during my time in England I was confronted repeatedly with the view that Christianity has no place in socialism. Throughout the article we have seen that there is a sense in which the Christian has no place here. He is merely tolerated in the hope that he will disappear as quickly as possible. Nevertheless, despite this and all the restrictions imposed upon our religious life in Romania, I claimed in England, in lectures given at many universities, that this is *not* true. We have a place in the socialist state. My reasoning was as follows. God is the One who decided that we live here in a country which became communist. He has revealed Himself to us and made us His children through the new birth here in a socialist country. We have not found Him, but He has found us. We have not chosen Him, but He has chosen us. Since, therefore, He chose us from *within socialism*, it means *He wants us here*. The very facts that evangelical Christianity prospers here in socialism, and that the numbers of believers are increasing fast, in spite of opposition, tell us that God is at work, at work with exceptional power. On the basis that God is taking the initiative I would give a decided yes to the question whether we have a place in socialism or not. *God* has given the Christian his place here, and if it is God-given then no one can deny it to him.

Besides, if God is the one who has set the Christian within socialism, it means He has a purpose for him, a mission to the socialist society which He has committed to his charge. What is God's purpose? We must recognise that God has replied to man's problems, both individually and socially, by giving His son, Jesus Christ. *He* is the solution, offered by God to mankind. He is God's unique and final response and He leaves us free to accept or reject Him. God offers this answer. This solution is His way for man and the socialist society to attain wholeness. The task and mission of the evangelical Christian is to present God's solution to mankind. The evangelical Christian is a Christ-bearer, one who reveals Christ and offers Christ to those around him. He does this joyfully, even if it brings suffering, discrimination, deprivation or even death.

The divine task of the evangelical Christian living in a socialist country is to lead such a correct and beautiful life that he both demonstrates and convinces this society that he *is* the new man which socialism seeks and desires. Evangelical churches in socialist countries are to produce these men of character which society needs. If they fail to produce such men, they have failed in their divine calling.

We observed that religion's disappearance within socialism has not happened, and that neo-protestant Christianity, a lively, dynamic, creative manifestation, has grown rapidly in the years under socialism. What does the Christian faith offer Romanian Socialist Society? Here is a tentative answer, in one direction only.

It is known that delinquency and crime is a growing problem in Romania. The Home Office (Procurator General) has commissioned many sociological studies in an attempt to discover the reasons for this alarming phenomenon. One such study was made of young people within the neo-protestant churches to see how much violence, lawbreaking, vandalism, thefts and killings were committed by the youth of these denominations. To the surprise of the researchers their findings were almost nil, whereas from young people in the rest of the country they collected some terrible statistics.

We must point out that these results, indicating the moral purity of neo-protestant youth, were achieved amidst all the difficulties encountered by the churches of these denominations. Officially the church is forbidden to carry out any education of its children or young people. What could these churches achieve if they were free to exercise fully their beneficial influence upon the morality of the young people? We are convinced that practical experience could produce miracles in this direction and that it would be of tremendous value to our socialist society as a whole.

Conclusion

The Socialist State is faced with a major problem. The phenomenon of religion is taking a deeper hold within socialism, and the neo-protestant denominations are growing. How will the State react? Every limitation of liberty within the neo-protestant churches, and all the pressures imposed on them, especially during the years 1948–1965, have not been able to stop their growth. A tightening of pressure and open persecution would have no other effect than to increase the zeal and passion of hundreds of thousands of believers. Only a general massacre, another 'St Bartholomew's Night', would break them, but not even this would entirely uproot them from the land.

We should bear in mind the advice offered by a member of the Jewish Parliament, the Sanhedrin, in Jerusalem, during a debate on the right attitude to be taken towards the early Christians. 'Men of Israel, take care what you do with these men . . . keep away from these men and let them alone; for if this plan or this undertaking is of men, it will fail; but if it is of God, you will not be able to overthrow them. You might even be found opposing God.' (Acts 5:35, 38, 39.)

It was this paper's main purpose to demonstrate that evangelical Christians are not harmful to socialism, but on the contrary, they are needed. They can offer a vital contribution to socialist society. Socialism has nothing to lose by giving them a try. Let the evangelical believer enjoy full religious freedom, treat him as a citizen with full rights and not simply as a tolerated person. Grant him the possibility to show that *as a Christian* he has something definite to contribute to society. In other words, let socialism give Christ a chance, give him a free hand to manifest his revolutionary and character-transforming power. Christ will carry through the most profound, wholesome revolution in this society. The Christ Revolution will meet the need of the socialist society.

Men who seek to transform the whole world need only fear Christ because He points out that this transformation must first begin within the very men who seek to transform the world. Revolution must start with ourselves and only He who loved mankind so much that He was prepared to be crucified for them can do this transformation in ourselves. Socialism needs the sacrificial spirit of Christ. Will it take up this offer? This is the major question to which we await an answer.

Other Marshall Pickering Paperbacks

THROUGH DAVID'S PSALMS

Derek Prince

Derek Prince, internationally known Bible teacher and scholar, draws on his understanding of the Hebrew language and culture, and a comprehensive knowledge of Scripture, to present 101 meditations from the Psalms.
Each of these practical and enriching meditations is based on a specific passage and concludes with a faith response. They can be used either for personal meditation or for family devotions. They are intended for all those who want their lives enriched or who seek comfort and encouragement from the Scriptures.

LOVING GOD

Charles Colson

Loving God is the very purpose of the believer's life, the vocation for which he is made. However loving God is not easy and most people have given little real thought to what the greatest commandment really means.
Many books have been written on the individual subjects of repentence, Bible study, prayer, outreach, evangelism, holiness and other elements of the Christian life. In **Loving God**, Charles Colson draws all these elements together to look at the entire process of growing up as a Christian.
Combining vivid illustrations with straightforward exposition he shows how to live out the Christian faith in our daily lives. **Loving God** provides a real challenge to deeper commitment and points the way towards greater maturity.

THE TORN VEIL

Sister Gulshan and Thelma Sangster

Gulshan Fatima was brought up in a Muslim Sayed family according to the orthodox Islamic code of the Shias.

Suffering from a crippling paralysis she travelled to England in search of medical help. Although unsuccessful in medical terms, this trip marked the beginning of a spiritual awakening that led ultimately to her conversion to Christianity.

Gulshan and her father also travelled to Mecca in the hope that God would heal her, but that trip too was of no avail. However, Gulshan was not detered. She relentlessly pursued God and He faithfully answered her prayers. Her conversion, when it came, was dramatic and brought with a miraculous healing.

The Torn Veil is Sister Gulshan's thrilling testimony to the power of God which can break through every barrier.

NOW I CALL HIM BROTHER

Alec Smith

Alec Smith, son of Ian Smith the rebel Prime Minister of Rhodesia whose Unilateral Declaration of Independence plunged his country into twelve years of bloody racial war, has written his own story of those years.

The story of his life takes him from early years of rebellion against his role as 'Ian Smith's son' through his youth as a drop-out, hippy and drug peddler into the Rhodesian forces.

A dramatic Christian conversion experience at the height of the civil war transformed his life and led to the passionate conviction to see reconciliation and peace in a deeply divided country.

What follows is a thrilling account of how God can take a dedicated life and help to change the course of history.

If you wish to receive *regular information* about *new books*, please send your name and address to:

London Bible Warehouse
PO Box 123
Basingstoke
Hants RG23 7NL

Name...

Address ....

....

....

....

I am especially interested in:
☐ Biographies
☐ Fiction
☐ Christian living
☐ Issue related books
☐ Academic books
☐ Bible study aids
☐ Children's books
☐ Music
☐ Other subjects

P.S. If you have ideas for new Christian Books or other products, please write to us too!